The DUN BOX

an essay in shades of no particular shade

Richard Fenton Sederstrom

Also by Richard Fenton Sederstrom

Fall Pictures on an Autumn Road

Disordinary Light

Folly: A Book of Last Summers

Eumaeus Tends

Selenity Book Four

Sorgmantel

Icarus Rising: Misadventures in Ascension

The DUN BOX

Richard Fenton Sederstrom

Published by the Jackpine Writers' Bloc, Inc.

Published by the Jackpine Writers' Bloc, Inc.
Edited by Sharon Harris
Layout and cover design by Tarah L. Wolff
Photography by Richard Fenton Sederstrom

Acknowledgments

The poet gratefully acknowledges the following magazines as the original publishers of the following poems:

The Blue Guitar Magazine: "The Dun Box," (early version of Part 3 of this book), "Far Shores Closing," (early version of Part 4 of this book), "Nimrod Stands By," "Sorting the News in America," "Xmas to Infinity."

Dissident Voice: "The Academics of It All," "All the Rules," "Am Now," "Flips," "Lightning Flash: A Strobe Dream," Lych Gathering," "Measureless Float," "A New Kind of Light Again," "Notes from the Heretic," "Real Notes."

The Talking Stick: "Familiar," "Leaflight," "Strange Landings," "When You Tease."

Unstrung: "A Brief Glamour of Time"(original title: *"a quelque point"*), "Flint Knapping," "Green," "Wake Robin," "William Duffy's Hammock Was Strung Between Two Trees."

And from earlier books, a group of poems who promoted themselves to be of new energy in new contexts: "Zhuang Zhou's Monkeys," the narrative parts of "A Brief Glamour of Time," "A New Kind of Light Again" having revised itself, "Note to the Office of Interpretation," "Words to the Orthodox," originally "Words with Heraclitus," "All the Rules," revised. Plus odd bits and lines here and there that refused to stay put, which are welcome, even for their resistance to being acknowledged further.

Dedicatory Acknowledgments

As Ever: to Sharon Harris and Tarah Wolff, who have cared for me and for my work through eight books now, for their professionalism, artistry, and poet-management. I've said before: "I don't know what relationships are like in the commercial publishing biz, and I don't care to know." With Sharon and Tarah at my back and by my side, I don't need to find out.

I continue to owe my debt of gratitude to Rebecca Dyre of *The Blue Guitar Magazine* and Angie Tibbs of *Dissident Voice* for their support of my experiments and eccentricities all these years. Becca has been especially supportive of my experiments, many of which she has been the first to publish, including nearly half of this book, in various forms.

Dedication

to Carol, for Carol

And again, again, after yet another two mad, infantile years of human-kind's continued drift towards . . . well, we shall hope the drift is only *towards*.

To our children, Carol's and mine, our grandchildren and our great-grandchildren, I wish you each, as last time, a full and peaceful life. More doubtful than the last time, I fear for you and for my wishes.

Again, this dedication expands: to the children of endangered generations that my generation will not live to feel for or continue to fail. The poems in this book, about human failures, intentional or not—about human delusions, sometimes intentional, about the only species to evolve on Earth likely to cause its own extinction, though unintentionally until very recently, and also about what I would miss should I live to that day or hour: Hugh and Vera Fenton, Zhuang Zhou, and the other friends of my centuries of reading and talk; some listening.

The good, corrective, news remains that, the folly of Anthropos not around to encourage its rampage, life will go on, probably in many, though more modest forms, evolution being the power that it has been these several eons. The New Eden of the Water Bear?

Contents

The DUN BOX

On the Death of Probability

"The Subjunctive Mood is seductive.
Most persons cannot begin
to acknowledge its authority,
even to admit a name for it.

Probability is the vice of the thinking class."

Stokhastes

Shepherds attend, your happyneſs who place
In gluttony alone, the ſwain's diſgrace;

. . .'Tis ours to ſpeak the truth in language plain,
Or give the face of truth to what we feign.

from Hesiod's *Theogony*,
trans. Thomas Cook, 1728
*   *   *   *

You Shepherds of woods and vales, shameful wretches,
empty bellies—
We know how to make lyrics of lies, pretend their truth.
Still, we also know when we choose, to sing what is.

Extracted version
for Eumaeus, Zhuang Zhou, Du Fu, Hugh Fenton
trans. rfs, 2021
*

"Se non è vero, è molto ben trovato."
Giordano Bruno
from *De gli eroici furori* [*The Heroic Frenzies*]

"Ma vale la pena bruciare?" Eumao

i Practice

Deep in the cave, the rising
fire of your torch ignites the eye of the aurochs

and she elects to move.
from *Sorgmantel*

Flint Knapping

Your left hand still bleeds.
A deep cut too, where
you held the flint.
You try hard to think
out the next strike.

You strike.
A shard flies.
It misses your eye. You
will flinch at the next strike.

After the decision,
practice is the error. Or
the decision was wrong.
Or only ill-timed.

       *

Don't practice.
Don't practice knowingly.
Do the thing for good.
Don't practice unknowingly.
Do the thing for good.

If you must do it over
and over again—
and you must—
do it now, each try,
and do it for forever—
until the next time.

       *

For some of us
these are our nights.
Surviving night
never abides practice.
                *

(The answer's always in the last few lines.
Unless it isn't.
To understand the answer,
the question is somewhere in the text.
Unless it isn't.

To understand the text, whatever the text may be—
pages in the book, bones in limestone strata,
drawing on the rock wall, the blood
smells breathed through the forest—read it.

Then think beyond it on your own.
Live your questions on your own.
When you've come to what you think is an answer:
lose the answer, remit the question,

and start over . . .
on your own,
but part of your own
is the company you let find you—)
            e, zz, tf, hdf, rfs

Zhuang Zhou's Monkeys

"This animal advertised his own cleverness.
He thought no one could touch him."
Thomas Merton's version

(1965)
Formless gray bug fumbles
into a corner of my eyeshot. I don't look.
I swat. It dies for its mosquito pretension.

Some admonition might Zhuang Zhou give here
casually to ward off disaster to the ambitious
from the shadow now of his westering way,
the crumpled silk of his small fame.

Will the next monkey to read Master Zhuang learn?
No. He will be hired as a prodigy to perform,
reading loudly to masses who will destroy him
in their envy, their formaldehyde admiration.

(1995)
A trophy fish, perfected in plastic
but surely not its old self, hangs high,
proud on a suburban wall, admired for size,
shades of color, poise of attack stroke
is nevertheless dead for the beauty endowed it.

Zhuang Zhou, poet of no size, shades of some one color,
poise of no attack, slips easily from the trophy wall
of my molded, shaded, buoyant, polystyrene
notions, all spaced in bucolic clutter.
And my own raw monkey-pelt?

7

(2015)
In my own way
I follow the master's indirection; avoid intent.

Pelt stretched here, wrinkled there,
balding and baggy-eyed, I have subtly avoided
the eight by ten glossy by way of the program
of unstudied inaction. But what about legacy?

Ah. Styles change.
What does the man of summer dao
know about the great world's taste
in the demimonde of monkeys?
Only, how to avoid that tree.

(2065)
Tree?

Lightning Flash, a Strobe Dream

Where can I sit now to sing new poems?
And beauty? Enchantment's finished at this thatch hut.
Du Fu

Another night.
Another night and another night
with more minutes than hours.

In weather like this, it seems
more hours awake than minutes asleep.

Wind and I are up together to answer male needs,
relieve the pressures of night on aging systems,
mine if not Earth's.

If Earth is tired as well
it may mostly be of me and of my human-kind.

Wind blunders around the dark
swinging lamp on the sleeping-porch.
Stumbles over my windowsill.

Wind and I blunder together toward the bathroom
but we glance outside.
If that ancient kindred jackpine snaps, shudders
cabinward, I need to see what happens. But

I don't want to be here when what happens
happens. Whether I see between lightning-strikes
or not—wind from the east—I'm his target.
But who is "He"?

Richard Fenton Sederstrom

My cabin is cousin to these pines,
the last of their race around my house—
cabin born of lumber slash and slash fire ashes,
all dying now out—for what does not?—
of senility aborning.

Pines of our cabin, the Folly,
are maybe a couple of generations older
than these loyal decrepit pines.
Maybe the Folly will protect me.

It has over and over again—
especially the thirty years I was elsewhere—
remembering, prodigal to our mutual care.
Kindredship blossoms with ages and space.

I hear, feel the soul-pine bend,
whip back and back and back again,
watch through a strobe light of lightning flashes.
Nature's manic kinetoscope wraith.

In the only second of perfect darkness
I hear the tree snap.
I look east toward the splintered dawn again.

And I am glad at what I cannot see beyond the lightning
or hear beyond the thunder to where some gods approach
through spattered darkness of their faulty invention.

Shadow deities loom gray through light invisible,
murky taupe of no dawn at all.
Toward me. Alone. And He? She?

10

The lightning? Wind? Fate?
The fierce wind bellows: the Aurochs.
She charges out from the east across the lake.

Or are my fiends and follies my self and soul alone,
with no more than night for company?
The storm I must have wished for.

Richard Fenton Sederstrom

Green

Mythic couples rehearse—millennia apart
to, with, Carol

We have been wed, you and I
not only together but with and into and . . .
and under now the leaf-kicked
tracks of the generations
we have longed again to re-create among the leaves.

We require no language outside our senses
sharing as we all do—
the two of us, the leaves,
the memories and the remembered
sound of yester-leaves crisp-crunching under foot.
We trail along after the heels of our fellow yester-persons.

The sight of leaves fluttering in front of, above us
and the dry smell of autumn
that we would not help but re-create to share
among us all—we, all who have so long now
"talked our extinction to death."

But we can afford to treat the issue gently
as our seemly gesture to Earth
until all are finally buried and mulched
under the last and heaviest snow- and foot-fall.

Now perhaps it might be courteous to live it lastly,
to learn to lie quiet, breathscape among shades.
Stubborn brown and rust of oak leaves
remind us of our familiar contracts,

or to abide by wisdom to restrain
the exhaustion of our winter distances.

I do not remember promising to return
to next year's falling shades.
But I have had occasions of longing in my autumn Folly
to have kept an imagined promise of staying.
  *

From first consciousness
we were brought to an edge of memory
in our neglected summers until
we learned out of time finally to enjoy among them
the return from green to gold, red, brown, yellow.
To green, like
  *

Penelope's live tree that found her way
into our garden, by its seed self-planted. We remember,
you and I wherever
  *

Persephone's red blossoms, the gift of her fruit to you,
your shared beads of pomegranate,
your gesture of our happy equality now
and in our strata of well-planted seasons.

A Brief Glamour of Time

It's about 10:48 by my grandfather's watch,
but we don't take him seriously in matters of time.
I said "him," my grandfather, Hugh Douglas Fenton.

When a friend asks for the time, he and I look sharp.
We offer a brisk answer, "10:48," preceded by
a tactful decorous unhurried "oh, about."

The truth as we read it, undisguised as fact.

A passing stranger asks for the time, and the two of us,
myself at the helm these many years past—
for sure, only by default—are politely circumspect.

"O, yes, I beg your pardon, but I have, oh, about
ten minutes to eleven," spoken in words, not numbers.
Time is elegant, like this clear lake,
a grace for language.

Far out from most strangers' time, we speak wraithsome
slow. We pace ourselves in conversation,
cadences angling toward poetry.

And to tell time accurately, or about,
I wind his watch, the rectangular Hamilton,
having looked at the heretical digital clock—

static, songless figures that would enumerate
beauty, regulate the asymmetric comfort of grain

in pine paneling, generations of story and dream,
ghosts on the wall.

Paterfamilias now, fellow phantom in training,
I set the dial of a watch that runs about a minute fast
to keep me, but not, I suspect, my grandfather, on my toes,

translating the wall clock's turgid demands
into the slow, miniature sweep
of the delicate millimeters of the minute hand.
                    *

             One hour proceeds to nothing but another.
We would prefer to live in the other.

             The hour that precedes does,
by something like definition,   m o v e .

             But in its office of preceding
it can move nowhere. By definition? By intuition?

             Perhaps the hour proceeds in time,
but with no object for the hour to proceed toward, time cannot move

so it cannot proceed.
             The next hour cannot come, cannot be,

nor can the object we cannot obtain, out of any time
that cannot be.

Something we want no more than to believe is "time."
But time is measured in static units, like the hour we search for.

If one hour proceeds, it maintains its own cell in time,
forcing ahead and ahead the time we would prefer to occupy.

The trepid empty feeling of knowing when we are:
we are in the only hour ever possible.

The next hour is no more than an idea.
But it is not an unworthy one. If not worthy,

then no worthy idea can ever be.
Still, with age

it becomes almost possible to bend,
if not the joints, time. But sadly, never in time.
        *

It is only in summer when Carol and I move
into my grandparents' old summer home—
gathered with ancestors, gathering with descendants—

that Hugh Fenton and I separate,
not far apart, and I get to listen
as a grandson again.

In summer our Hamilton stops on us
with significant regularity.
I sit at the dock in my idle rowboat and hear

Whatever do you need a wristwatch for in summertime?
Anything pressing just now?

The Dun Box

If I might make a small recommendation,
I suggest that you leave the watch in the cabin,

take your boat out onto the lake and fish.
And remember to hold your mouth right.

I am willing to compromise, always have been.
I keep the watch on my wrist, so as not to mislay it.

But instead, I find myself reminded of odd passing debts
I may or may not owe somewhere to anyone, and I will pay
    *

gladly and alone for the pain of learning what I have been
by struggling to adapt to what I may become.

So, weaned memory-long from præpotent faith,
yet always gnawing septic self-chastisement,

to survive I inhale the least quantum
of the breath I write to feel:

in words I confront
an infinity of possible Feynman diagrams.

Ink-brushed characters sway in Blue Cliff Record
where kaon meets koan, nohwhere.

Looking back up, I step back down.
Sine proprio,

Richard Fenton Sederstrom

I pause to look in the direction of a pine-shaded kaon
cooling its feet in a sacred mountain stream, invisible in dao.

I rub the stubble of my beard to wake the rest of me
and I wonder all about, inviting an apposite koan.
                    *

            for Bartleby, 167 years after his invention
            of Herman Melville

But what's in all this for the poet? Ah.
The Auction—*Disgrace of Price.*

I would prefer not to; I think,
time

following or,
ocean permitting,

            washed away
to some last time drowning all, *and* time.
                    *

But not to drown, not just yet, and to keep
the conversation going I do take the boat out onto the lake,

keep the old timepiece dry in my tackle box,
plunk a lure of some sort idly into the clear water.

Admire the poetry of the sky.
Then I wobble my lips and scrunch my face.

The Dun Box

My grandfather would tell me again to:
"Hold your mouth right," and I will,

or I will try, oh,
in good time, surely.

Richard Fenton Sederstrom

XMAX to Epiphany

Is it the twelfth day?
On the final long, long day
toward the hazel-colored western horizon—
after the short rest comes the long disillusion.

The toys under the tree have lost some shine.
The track for the electric train doesn't quite connect.
Needles fall into broken ornaments.

One pigskin glove of the pair that signified
a step toward unmittened manhood
has been lost in some closet,
or somewhere in the snow,
some erased spot, threateningly sacred now,
dedicated to the discovery of dismay.
        *

Our relationship with the elements
of the quantum universe is the adult view
of our relationship with the gods we carve,
but still ephemeral almost to the fine point
of the paradox of empty space
from atom to axiom and back
to a graphite smear on the retina.
        *

In our institutional crusade for exactitude,
for the purity of the Absolute,
the liege of Corporate Capital Law,

we have long stopped extolling beauty, failing
even to reckon with the callous and tawdry.

Still, some struggle for beauty, or
shadow of beauty, echo of beauty,
cobbled rubrics
that conjure and curate the beauteous
according to patent law and copyright.
    *

What a wonder of imagination!
that having discovered that we can't control what is—
the tides, the weather,
the migration of wildebeest,

the behavior of our children or the clan in the next forest,
the vatic fecklessness of poets—
we turn to a faith in our power to control
what we know to be ephemeral,

a hopeward *confessio fidei,*
or a dire cauldron of narcotic lies—
canticles from the Gospel of Goebbels
or the Tweet of Trump, Putinspit,
the hateward liturgy of penance enforced.
The deathward legacy of bondage.
    *

We search through any bright rubble,
explain, explicate, elucidate, elude—
ensepulcher the ramble of discordant minds,
write into the orthodoxy of Babel

but only partway in,
no farther than the orotund preambles.

We eschew the desperate agony
of questioning into the still-wrenching
insights of axial thinking, the luminous
agon, searching some onset of awareness,
without which we listen for beauty —
while we record dis-chord.

But for a few, if only a few for now,
if only for the day, especially for the day,
the horizon remains horizon,
whatever range and color, whatever distance.
And rest is rest whenever we can get it;
sleep comes sometime, and it *is* sleep,
no matter what we may be bound to dream in it.

                *

The toys have so long gone that their color is restored
now and then when the dream is right.
And the train,
which I did find in one closet or another,
sat on a window ledge for years
until I noticed that the sun had faded it on one side.

So I keep that side to the sun
and let another dream repair as it may,
and the great black engine stands by, chuffing —

my dreamt soul, heavy-gauntleted,
in control in the iron cab, the chrysalis

The Dun Box

I know I must moult from when I grow up,
steaming now at the speed of history
from coast to eternity.

It's also my choice to declare with quiet Bartleby
"I would prefer not to," orphaned at last
and knowing that the sea rolls on.
        *

It's not that I have missed that glove, of course.
But I would still miss the sense of the loss
at times when I am inclined to miss
all the other frustrations
and embarrassments and losses.

I would miss especially the memory
or even the sad elation at being able to remember.
Some joy too,
that frisks along behind, dependably
in the little red caboose of late and early memory.

I think of the glove
and still regret that, even with a new pair,
my mind was fixed,
still mittened for a time, as it is just now,
for a time.

The spot in the snow, grown over and over,
the place I never did find,
is still sacred though, to my discovery
of the virtue of dismay,
and the pain of all such future discoveries

and the still sad music that should remain.
I register the notes again in my brain's second ear.
                *

Mendelssohn's Sixth String Quartet, his last,
someday maybe my last too,
in its pain of unspeakable grief,
of rage at the loss of love and of self-hope,

and a daemonic need to resist reconciliation
and accept in the beauty of the quartet
what one death forecasts to another,
the composer's, who died at just half my age.
So, the old poet too, perhaps.

We, but how many are we?,
in willful thrall to the music, struggle our way
not to peace, but toward tomorrow,
the thirteenth day.
But now the sun is back out.

The late-day sun shines out the adagio
of branch-latticed snow, chanceled light
for a motif to introduce the physics,
the gravity of theme

in the place we need revealed to us
for no longer than the hours
when the music and the silence swell
to become a return to the first moments of sharing—

the composer, the poet, the gift of
the music, the words, a concerto
of distant figures in time:

mouths, ears, wood, sinew, pen and ink—
hands working in the clays of notation.
Tools to create the fulfilled hours,
the newborn rhythms of the pliant, mortal day.

Richard Fenton Sederstrom

Sorting the News in America

He jokes.
He asks, "Have we made any lately?"
He means "news."

She reminds him that news is made by people
in position to make news,
whether they want to or not.

And a few minutes later, she adds
"and if they don't want, someone else might,
in spite of themselves or their desire for privacy.
Like our desire for privacy, your desire and mine.

Like people from those cold and barren places—
OK, even places that are warm and crowded—
where in their yearly winter starvation
they sent word out to lure each other
as the prime entrees in the wet red ink
on the carnal menu.

Well, other animals, of course.
Not people, I mean. No, not people.
We may want to make news or not, you and I,
but we're the sort who like to keep it to ourselves."
　　　*

They are modest by nature and desire.
They are growing old.
So maybe it doesn't matter what private news
they may make before they forget it anyway.

The Dun Box

*

Tweet-free, real news stays news somewhere maybe,
but as driven motes in a gale,
and as mutely shared as dreamt and undreamt myth,
ours to share or not to share to no ear in hearing.

After all, it may be a poem and it may be written
as a poem, unless it is whispered.
Some things can only be whispered.

The poem, uttered as stammers of breath
or coded chthonic echoes, lies somewhere
in what we can't hear from the people outside
when we choose to escape from who can't hear or won't.
And then they speak loud, those people,
whether they utter real words or not.
*

"And you look at what my fingers say
when they touch, caress your lips."

"The police?"
is what the silent fingers ask
in soul-remembered fragments
of ancient, righteous primate fear,
through which we become the other animals—

Leaflight
for Carol

We walk the Folly road again
with purpose-seeming steadiness
until we reach the deeper ruts,
the road-side windbreaks and obstacles—
trodden crumbling emblems of the continents of time.

Hummocks and ruts serve to catch and hold
the first wind-blown leaf-fall: maple, birch, aspen.
We also catch at the falling leaves,
as many as we can hold away from their fate.

We hold the leaves in the outside hands,
the hands that aren't holding each other,
children's hands again.

Then, children for only another vapor of breath,
we toss leaves: maple, birch, aspen,
until we are covered like Egyptian birds
painted in titanium iridescence.
                    *

Without feet leaving the path
we rise in our sheen of leaves and fly
into the freedom—

rarer, shorter each year now—leaves
Claret and Rhenish, well-aged life
in the colors of wine.

You gesture a silent trick of question
and I ask where.
You beckon to show me.

ii Notes from the Course and Flow

The generations of the bird are all
By water washed away. They follow after.
They follow, follow, follow, in water washed away.
    Wallace Stevens, "Somnambulisma"

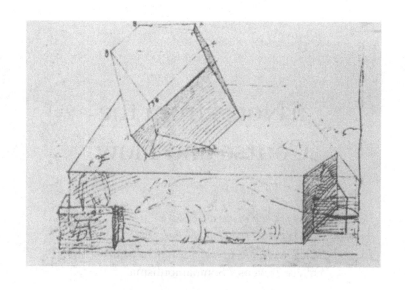

drawing for Abrecht Dürer's Melancholia I

Course: an essay on cultural tectonics—
building, pressure, fault

Lych-Gathering

Protecting her young of some species,
a mother at the beach leaves the corpses of biting flies
scattered on a deck beneath her.

Unwittingly I wish for the ghost of Matthew Brady,
the ghost and the ghost's chimerical camera,
the ghoul-worthy who might render annihilation

in the iron bas-relief photogravure
and proto-gravitas,
lines

of blackened corpses swept off
the deck, sinking
Styxward into obsidian depths.

The dead remain remembered only
in the media-driven catafalque below headlines,
the legacy of passing insult.

The species turns almost human, the mother,
the young, the flies. But first and finally
we all tumble and rust into the cold magic of glass plates—

from *Sorgmantel:*

Eurydice alive
Orpheus cannot contemplate death.
Without the contemplation of death
the necessary urgency of poetry,
enchantment
remains stillborn.
And poetry with it.
          *

The irony in speaking of war
is that there is no irony in speaking of war.
War is too reptilian for irony.

Peace is the playground of irony
which happens after the blood has petrified
into the innocent sentimentality of Epic

after the poet has dared to return to the people of the hearth —
the warmth of creative peace that is expected to demand
again the hearth-rending culture of war, because

the great emotions are lacerating.
We want to demand of the epic that it tether the emotions so
that we can ride them like ponies.

Ride and dream.
Whirl around on the merry-go-round.
Dizzy the reel from ground to grail . . .

to grave:
the
American Century

Which began on 2 September 1945
Ended 25 days *earlier,*
Starting already in arrears—

From time
out of mind to mind out of time,
those arrears would appear
impossible to redeem or dream.
Redemption requires intention and time.
*

The nation has been time out of its mind from the start,
nightmare opiated into Disney™©fied dream,
metavirtual since Lexington and hype-blissed history—
glamour-smashed and stoned into its scripture.
*

Ninth August Nineteen Hundred and Forty-Five,
Date of the First Official Gesture
of the Appearance of the Epoch Anthropocene:
Omnicide.
* * *

Catun si fascia di quel ch'elli è inceso
Dante, *Inferno*, Canto xxvi

. . . the poet's traditional living between
the shaman and the scientist
participating at the extremes
as intermediary and as interlocutor.

The living demands the natural
which attempts to unite the extremes —
which are not really extremes anyway

but life between the inhalations and the exhalations,
the verbs that give resonance to long-held breath.

For when we hear the still small voice
it isn't a god we hear.
It is ourselves.
It isn't a god we hear, small, insignificant, powerless.

It is ourselves, small, insignificant, powerless.
It is the voice of the silent passing wing.
It is Everyvoice in our chorus of wuthery breaths.

I am looking at the wound
sometimes from the inside
and I want my work to let out the new wild —

Illusion, Delusion: *Ilume* 1

Lines from only two books ago,
do you remember, poet?
You will hear yourself later,
from Dickinson's prompting,
a perverse inversion:
Belief is a capacity of physics,
the sacred illume of doubt.

Hold to that, old man, because otherwise
what world is this in which or what of how many
finite dimensions of physics and an infinite
chthonic first mammalian imagination, twinned,
seeming cacophonous for now or ever,
your own ever, certainly,

and in this range of time and dimensions
and ghosts—the Aurochs herself!: your *ain ma*.
When and where remains or will reappear
a rug by the fire for the poet?

Step softly and grope. Be quiet about it.
The darkness is not your only blindness.
Not entirely. *Carpe lucem ex tenebris.*
Pluck gently and strain the light.
Decant your vision.
Your pen's on the desk. Use it—
                    *

A first stumble, then, by way of moral:
I hope that as a people we will be remembered
by what we deserve to be remembered.

37

As a Nation we certainly will be. I hope not
to live to be a chewed morsel of our
well-deemed requital, *quidpro quo stultitia.*

As a People?
Well, if we dare continue . . .
Deacon Lawrence still makes his joke on the gridiron.
        *

Ett Eden är deras död
*där jaktdjurens andar går i bet**
            Gunnar Ekelöf

*Their death is an Eden
where the spirits of beasts of prey go to graze

                        trans. Leonard Nathan and James Larson

Flips

Fall is upside blown—sere, like humanity these days,
like evolution's other playthings—
maples partly rust-red, more like oaks but mostly still green,
and the oaks, usually the last to color, now the first,
all mummified into a dull fossil brown.

Some trees are bare as February,
some green as August.
Which month comes first in our missing todays
in a blind future extrapolated
from seasons of dis-ease?

What season has not skewed to another ghost of expectations?
The human mind is a glass-bead bauble:
but also a fine-knapped obsidian scalpel—
texture and obscure brightness to lure the touch of hands,
an obsidian blade shaman-knapped,

so sharp that we will feel no sense of the cut
until we think to look down
at the silence of gently flowing blood.
Some fault in the edge is necessary
to make the touch a gesture of remembering—

Where We Lived Then

In Granite Falls on that September second
my mother ended her homebound celebration.
She returned to the summons of my baby brother Jackie,
a month old now plus three days.

I don't know where my father was. Handicapped
and 4F, he celebrated both victory and relief for a man
who had spent the war humiliated at having survived,
a lifetime victim of conscience. Now . . .

Now I have lived almost four score years in a nation
whose talent is to forget the things that *did* happen
and remember . . .
well, . . . Well? . . . Remember? :
           *

In Nagasaki
Sadako Sasaki died ten years later of leukemia.
She was twelve. Dying,
she learned the legend of the cranes. She folded 644 of them.

Her friends finished her goal of 1,000 cranes
after Sadako had fled into the bright paper of birds.
We cannot know what wish it was the task fulfilled.

After the atomic bomb explodes, what agency
is it that burns the flesh of children? Is it the plutonium?
Or is it the credulous virtuosity of politicians?

So much we do not know about chosen tasks,
about cranes, about why children die.
We know how Sadako died, and before her

as many as 32 percent of Nagasaki's population—
family, friends, futures.
The *hibakusha* numbered 189,163. Some survive—

to cancer, birth defects, barbarities to body and mind.
What we do not know we can conceive. Or we cannot.
Bikini Atoll. Utah. Earth. Keep tally. Does tally dare exist?

At 1,000 *orizuru* for each wish, one *senbazuru*,
each death—each wish for one thousand
orizuru, one's own release to fly orbits round a universe?
                    *

In 1945 my grandparents bought a summer shack on a lake.
I have lived almost as long as any male in the family
since Francis Fenton, born 1690, died in his ninetieth year.

I still own the place, Fentons' Folly.
Note to tallykeepers: humans tally large, but
as around the world, birds sing in growing peril.
                    *

One fall morning we stopped on the side of County Road 4
to watch the first pair of sandhill cranes we'd seen here ever.
We had not anticipated hearing them though.
It is a life-rattle sound. It was echoed
in the wooded distance across the road.

The echo was quieter, the same notes but shriller,
and we chose to follow slowly on the two-rut track
that led into a dark cluster of pines. We did not find
the new-fledged bird in hiding, of course, and we are still
moved that we did not hear it again. We hear it now.

My memory is allowed to expand. Expanding,
my expectations for the species, including our children,
grandchildren, great grandchildren, and the chance
of descendants to match ancestors in number, contract
according to each dire consequence of human genius. Yours?
　　　*

Climate, pandemic, war,
corruption, depression. Delusion.
News that stays for seconds in the distracted psyche.

Has our world together become so tedious
in just that time, and does shared tedium
make us worthy to tweet virtual prophecy?

. . . when our ambition rises to the massy height
of listening finally, well, and in submissive quiet . . .
but since and now, here alone in time, as always
victors drift from the pain of their victims.

Once more:
There is no irony in speaking of war.
War is too reptilian for irony.

The Dun Box

Have we lived at all, outside
the bubbles of our servile delusion?
No? Then learn to live once for all—
     *

Once, maybe 1,500 generations or so ago,
we waited with our mothers outside by a fire.
We waited for the men, the man with the bent finger,
whose signature has drifted into the generations.

They came out of the cave in silence.
In the same silence they passed us.
They walked into the dark to wait the night out.
No one spoke. We felt hunger. For a time.
We looked into the fire.

We rise into the dark.
We open the other senses.
Regard horizons from the forest's edge.
Circle the habitat.
     *

Now, entrepreneurs of virtual history,
we treat invented time, the incorporeal predicate
of existence, as though it can be purchased
on credit and paid in bitcoin—

Where We Live Now

Nimrod Stands By

One of these days
Rod will throw this broken Adirondack chair away.
Just drive it to the dump
where it will be shopped off into some new use:
a chair again maybe.
Or maybe only the honest junk
it has worn to be.

But for now he thinks he can't
because all that remains of it to his possessive eye
is the shotgunned gap in the chairback
that he blasted
when he only grazed the red squirrel.

He didn't much want to hit the squirrel anyway.
Much. Only scare him
from this neighborhood of nests
full of songbird eggs and baby birds.

The squirrel jumped to the cabin roof,
nursed his stinging leg
and laughed at Rod
for turning this chair that neither wanted
into a shrine to the squirrel's memory
and Rod's embarrassment.
A chair he can't sit in anymore—
won't, nor get rid of
for its sinister image of inept wanton humanity.

An American abashed,
Rod will stand back
and Rod will stand by
to practice his failing aim
and savor the palate of his rage —

Rod's ordained rage: Rod thinks
of his President, elected once —
then self-anointed for the Ages.
Rod's simple Ages.
All oaths kept: Fire!

Flat Earth Hermitage

It has been more than a year now of adventures in
      solitude.
Fifteen months? And on?
And what months to go? And go for gone?
Let us be resigned, however.
Ours is only a bit part in the long history of dis-ease.

Still, in my security
I don't have to step out of the house,
don't even have to look out the window,
when sometimes it seems I have walked
off the edge of Earth.

I'd have to look out the window, though,
to see the path in front of me.
Instead, I dream an old LP onto the turntable—
Bach's Violin Partitas and Sonatas—

the aural geography of an enlightened
cosmos I have almost escaped into:
a moon-calm trail,
sane to every sense with which

we learn to probe the quantum wholeness
of insanity.

The Academics of It All

> *All but Death, Can be adjusted*
> *Dynasties repaired —*
> *Systems — settled in their Sockets —*
> *Citadels — dissolved —*
> Emily Dickinson

Out of a deep time and time ago,
another abrupt transition:
transitionless transition to be uncertain,
to render a Cosmos chastely defined.

They matter little, any of these transitions,
in a world out of transition,
skewed toward extinctions,
one soggy bawling flop
of tantrum after another.

And promises:
soothing plots and righteous lies, human delusion —
self-delusion —
the astrolabe of mirage that clears to a mappemonde
hand-illuminated in the shipwrecked brain,

if we may re-compose any theme
wave-swept into some greater form
like the sea-beast that warns us what's uncharted
in the mind, our escape from linear
reality to re-join our fellow mammals.
                    *

Vitiate the vitiation of history.
Blind mouths! What we explain we confuse.

What we confuse we charge our poor wits to revive:
That curse!

Truth cannot be un-poetic, *I fondly*
dream, fondly misattended.
Doglike I would circle the cosmic habitat—
When I turn round from checking
the geography of dark space

I am cheered by the sight of Earth,
my guide to the mooncalm trail of stardust
behind me. I would probe
the hopewise cosmic wholeness of inner selenity.

Perhaps Lucretius?:

Clinamen—a swerve of the verse out of mind—
a furrow: verse being the expected and consistent flow
and turning among the furrows—
clinamen exposing the soil of natural tensions,
exposing both the tensions and the (poetic as well?)
consistency, of contention and release,
an eons-long drama of entropies
reflecting the constant relieving of tensions
and the constant tensing of every relief.
Verse and reverse, the turning of furrows,
time/space in lines of not yet written probabilities.

A Late Nudge from the Heretical Tradition
for John Duns, OFM re: *Haeccietas*

1. A Physics of Intelligence

This should not be easy. What we struggle
to learn and live of reality should not be easy.
Life is difficult, and life is confusing.
Should careful regard of life be other
than difficult and confusing?
What thing owns the answers? The clock?

And who deserves more than a poet
to live out among answers in nebulae than those
who are confused and who are fools enough
to acknowledge the difficulties? Well, who?

The first speaker of the new
will not have discovered the language
of clear answers. The first speaker must
search for the first ear: the second speaker.

Of a first speaker, Brother John:
> *Each mortal thing does one thing and the same:*
> *Deals out that being indoors each one dwells;*
> *Selves — goes itself; myself it speaks and spells;*
> *Crying What I dó is me: for that I came.*
>> Gerard Manley Hopkins,
>> a second speaker for John

Look back before, beyond beginnings.
Re-evolve, in lithic *bas relief. This* rock, incarnation

after incarnation of life like us turned limestone.
Eons of mute souls fossilized
reincarnate, replicate in evolving strata.
The negative soul a hardly destructible quantum fossil.

My preference will be to drift my ashy way
out of the crematorium as an act more far-drifting quantum
than the mud of grave-rotting—
but time is blunt punctuation in a photograph.

In the painting time performs as the predicate,
enveloping a never quite finished argument
of interior drama, cellular, in its own passing—organic,
asking for the gentle touch of the eye as of the hand,

and though mud is something organic anyway,
the ooze primordial soothing once again
and a pregnant fen of nebulae for something raw
to start from again again again again—

I'd prefer microbe or electron, or some choice:
one, other, both, neither—quark certainly,
but always something, all teasing toward life,
limbo, bardo, or dimension, imagination,
pneuma, ruah, aliento: the next new breath.

The Dun Box

2. Does Artistry Occlude Intelligence?

I long to regard Bartleby's determination—that is,
I would prefer not to, but would anyway
"write only in response to the gods."

Robert Lowell assists:
"universal consolatory description without significance
translated verbatim by my eye,"

the poet's aspiration to write, to live beyond language:
touch the black flint of hardened runes
that soften in proximity of your eye
distracted by clouds dappling some morning sky.
          *

Ann Berthoff stopped our conversation then.
"You are a poet," she said. "You don't
write in metaphor. But you are a poet."
          *

(Biographical: a poet's physical qualities)

Haceceitas: This pair of eyes. *Your* eyes.
This duck, a goldeneye. This very pond.
This very pond cooling to the body under this summer sun
on this, *this: this!* day:

upon which: our four—five?—voices
in their cacophonic concerto, ask "Of what? *that?*
Ask. But what *this?* Which *This?*

51

Hæcceitas, up until, that is, the saying, and the writing.
Evolution: does artistry occlude intelligence?

Then one moment *this* disappears, goes away awry.
So far awry that away no longer means.
Surpass the mere poem!: the clockwork.

Train to take sky, somewhile to wonder through the stars
for a brief landing, waking only to respond
under the surface of the lake, maybe to loon-call.

And then to surface, rise through schools of small dark fish,
white bellied above you like pubescent moons.
Allow for the Moon's cold gravity and pale welcome.

Then to sit up in the narrow field of the bed,
to watch the wakened stars framed by tree-shadow,
the faint new ones from the edge of the galaxy.
Study the cave wall for its map. Ask Night Bear.
        *

I remind myself that I have never had a falling dream.
It is only gravity that threatens distant accidents.
But gravity streams are easy to choose and control
for the conscientious dreamer. Again:
Surpass the mere poem! But listen.

Or don't. Not to me, a worn sear — monk-like:
the verge escapement that stops the word
for idle exhibition. Like this museum piece.
Only open your ears as far inside as you can.

It may be the first time your new-fledged deity
says (without saying until you do) "Come find me."
The elohim have disappeared, of course.
Into whom they have disappeared—
you and they whisper together.

You will no longer discover *this* or *away* or even *awry*
until you fail to remember that you need no longer look,
will no longer remember forgetting:

"Like Mallarmé who had the good fortune
to find a style that would make writing impossible."
This folly I would prefer because
there's room enough somewhere—*ubitas*—
room enough for me to invest in some,
what? gods? cultures out of time? Re-
invent what I won't invest of the rest of myself?

What is accidental and exterior I can remodel to be deific,
permanent because only momentary,
safe to the static imagination, like:
The Ocean. No Metaphor!! *Ocean*. But then,
expand to the elegant among sounds, out of control:
The Great River to the Source of Currents.

Gently, dissociate Stevens's *Ocean* from *Bird*—
they reflect the common force. Still, they are not,
cannot be, must never be pledged as one,
each disembodied thereby.

But they never can be other than One,
the one necessary image, invisible,

53

indivisible and concordant:
wing and wave, harpoon and ghost,
industrial America and chthonic Moirai
propelled from the same evolved breastbone:
Earth's. *Follow after*, but after what?
Mad prophet? Hallowed monster?

In the difference, defining inseparable from same:
only the scholar is separate,
necessarily so as well to the image—
of Everything Else, como el Desierto de la Sonora:
after a quail note out of the silent desert
into no more than the silent desert.

One and separate, they are hot fast blood to cold still depth—
Ahab and Whale: one felt only nearby,
one seen distantly until clash and mating: with death.

                    *

Lucretius plans the particulation of the Objective Void.
incommunicado and alone for a new start,
with how many billions of galaxies to wonder about in,
maybe more and more, the whole
filled with dimensions: replete with Form
but nothing void.

The Real Plot:
Pip's Caul/Budd's Stammer/Bartleby's Silence
(Biographical: a poet's inner qualities)

Not this hand complies with my humor
more genially than that boy — Ahab

Life buoy, sir. . . . Oh, look, sir!

The birds!   The birds!   I

    stammer   uh

            uh   toward . . . into . . .

Toward thee I roll,

        my own shadow,

            fading phantom

and avoid the epode

as I avoid finality,

      which I would   puh'   prefer . . .

        yes . . . ?

   or not

      to . . . ?

note:

the sea . . .

shroud . . .   caul . . .

I have said all,
Sir

?

dissolves with

Dong,

ding   dong

d'd'd'ding!

Who's
        seen Pip?
                Shame . . .

Shame on all cowards!

I hear ivory

cold   cold
        too dark

thus endeth

[n' n'. . . n'ever . . .]!

What can be the lure of that book?

?   under . . . but wait, wait for . . .

Disillusion: *Illume* 2

1
Den tredje hjärna
        för Göran Sonnevi

The third brain, the scholar-critic,
vox civilis, probing labyrinthine echoes of lost last lore
and the eye assessing the shade of the moving finger
in the dark. The bent finger,
the signature we invent in tutored retrospect.

The scholar's work is to discriminate our mysteries
into discrete parts, currents, tributaries
for observation and analysis, following after,
explicating and deconstructing,
dis-worded lyrics left bare-bottomed,

un-suckled and dumb—
by Nature and graced by reason, meaning.
But still, but still, those Mysteries left orphaned
and naked are always to be tended, nourished and given
to new language in fresh voices,

refreshed silences washed away.

: The crafted rest
preludes consummate symphonics.
It is the promise of awe eternal for
a fulsome earful of virtual sublime.

Ask of Creation in the long and holier rest

after the dark and prayerless silence
after the symphony's funeral resignation:
What is more immense than the First Quark
blinking on the sunny side of nothing at all?

2
Den första hjärnen, ensam

In lithic simplicity
I am joined to the dead of the city, and surrounds
near and far—Ithaka, Tempe; seas, plains, deserts—
we, unnamed soon or now,

the first brain, alone,
ghosts in common destruction, fossilized
clots of ash molded into the staggered footprints
of tear-drunken grave diggers.

Nagasaki and its dead might be the principal
unacknowledged haunters of our hubris-aborted American
Cenotaph. But we have forgotten when we fail to know.
                    *

Suicidal lies,
        so foul a thing . . .
such a question of such future as—
as, where shall we find a secure bridge?
Where shall we find a bridge so secure
that we can drive over it and not be distracted
by the knapped shine on the dark river below,

the river we cannot see through concrete and rails
but which we might see if we dare stop the car
and look down through the broken concrete
of our surfaces.

We might see the river between ledges of concrete
framed by rusting rebar.
But we will not stop.
We may be followed tonight.
We have been followed all day so far and so far.

Ah well.
We know that we will be followed tonight
and that we will still and ever be followed.
Followed. Followed, we drive.
We drive only as fast as our cracking surfaces allow us.

We drive steady.
We will leave the bridge in time maybe
to leave the car and walk below—
beneath the bridge where we may be secure.
In our breath of security we will lie beneath the bridge.

Before we sleep we will look up into the stars
framed by the rotting concrete and rusting rebar,
and we will pray to dream
that we do not see the surface

begin to crumble down,
begin to be trampled

by the machines and boots that will inaugurate
the heartbeat and throb of our new . . . our new . . .
security.
          *

And where is some mooncalf clodpole
far-gone-daft enough, some slapstick jester,
interlocutor or dumbstruck shaman blind enough
to dare look into that physics and breathe

the blue notes of imagination,
pure oxygen toward its crackling incineration:
unthought and wordless paean to
the pure peace of fire?

Am Now

> *"Eater, become food,"*
> Frank Bidart, "The Third Hour of the Night"

He thinks:
The dragonfly larva
is not a young dragonfly.
It is a different life.
The larva cannot fly.
The imago cannot swim.

He wonders:
Am I
just for now
the larva of a man? Not a younger man
but a reassembling being, here—now
new above the forgotten lakebed.

And thinks:
Will I
after my wings have dried
and after my eyes have re-collected
their multiverse lenses and focused into bright sync,

will I
having looked about
into the windblown green and hungry
interstices of Something's new world,

will I
when I am finally ready to leave
the surface of my dead life, become not the man

that has been me but newly constructed?
A fresh creation?

Will I
discover a bright new world into which I dare
take web-laced wings to the sky
or reveal a great Appetite
into which I may wobble for a few ravened hours?

Among the Poets of Mountains and Rivers,

I could go a thousand miles east
riding on my high spirits
skimming along in the shade of the mountains
aboard a simple skiff
                    (Du Fu)

or canoe, perhaps, after the perilous joy of . . .

... Flow: an essay on sedimentary erosion

But I'll rest up on the boat.
Hart Crane, letter to Bessie Meacham Crane, 4/22/32

Emily Dickinson:

The abdication of Belief
Makes the Behavior small—
Better an ignis fatuus
Than no illume at all.

belief *is* a capacity of physics,
the sacred illume of doubt.

Once Was an I

1. Henry's De-Solace-ion

> *"There is no me. I do not exist. There used to be a me... . . .*
> *but I had it surgically removed."*
>   Peter Sellers, *The Muppet Show*, 2/25/78

Heraclitus wrong, awry we reck him be,
complains again:
> *Now we can travel anywhere!*
> *no longer must we lug the poets*
> *and mythmongers along for stubborn witness*
> *about indisputable certainties.*
Manifest dogmatizing:
Ol' 'Enry Helleycat cannot help but prove
his poesy pitfall pudding.

But I need devise a rise of Other topography, Aether,
for my day's mothflight mythy purpose—
solve and prove the mph, the oomph
of a drive just three weeks ago
from one great river back to a nether—

but I must dive deeper than Google delves
for the wormhole-dimensional map we need.
Heraclitus, long witherstanding, I say otherwhile:
poets and physicists must and do drive to discover
the necessary dimensions and mis-dimensions:

Here, whence
all have departed or will do, here airless, where
the witchy ball

65

wanted, fought onward, dreamed of, all a green living
drops limply into one's hands
without pleasure or interest* [DS 19]
          *

like the watcher of the spinning
innards of the quarklike kaleidoscope
where we will re-define The Old Western Desert,
the desert that shall, so rock-re-defined, despite,
to spite us one fine domesdæġ

to end sinuous in spinous cacti at the Mississippi,
dragged and disappearing darkscape
in noun-free void behind the crumpled bumper, rear,
of our '54 Chevy cyclotron coupé,
oxidized. Leper-Blue.

Louisiana Purchase shore across Rice Street
and the current or the toboggan track of ice
20 miles upstream from Henry's
swansong and dive:
Jive, Mister Bones.
          *

Anne Bradstreet requited the heart,
the homage of Henry not at all. So:
385] in four hundred and twenty-nine dream songs
 44] and one flight of swan song
429] Henry committed his bridge jump
 1] four hundred and thirty times.
430] Every time his very last.

Can Henry live forfeiting Anne?

In the rain of pain & departure, still
Love has no body and presides the sun,
and elfs from silence melody. I run.
Hover, utter still,
a sourcing whom my lost candle like the firefly loves [HMB 57]

for in the adventure of dotage
I had forgotten A for the three of us;
but, Henry,
is A to us Anne?
we, both old, new-found and foundering?

He, not Henry, who is Was—
Is, less "I Am that I Am" than
"I Am as I Am . . . Was," omni-nihil,
which ain't misfortunate—apt-modest anyway,
for the guy who needs it most: MODESTY!   :

GRANDÉ HUMILITATÉ!—where,
in which state, de-solaced,
most of us are obliged to live but not quite
always—
all of us sometimes.
                    *

We sense a decreation do we?
age and the deaths and the ghosts [DE, p.40]
of part and part somehow leading to
equilibrium or dawn-ripping sunrise,
passing in such fastlessness

the mossy rim of the bright-shadowed well
right to sunset so very quicklike like life. . .
but it's too fraught
with so many perils leading nowhere—
now-where?—

as sweeping as Yeats
but without those artificial fundaments,
gilded fowl solid as metaphors
swathed in ether
but no Byzantium tessellated, gilt,

outside-inside-outside tinsel-tiled
eternal spin in slippage:
only the naked soul of poet, busy,
epicbrained or eddafied, size or horizon
relative to observation, relativicity:

quarks in quanta.
Poets carve diversions in dimensions,
re: disturbed dimensions,
multiplex spooks in tesseract Salem,
multidimensionally gabled. And yet,

but yet, garbled too, there's
poetry and scholarship,
lorn and together longing,
lunemad Henry's worser mixed-drink drug:
academic luminary longing—for a Brother Hood.
        *

The Dun Box

Is it because of the common dependence
and competition on and on with words that
seem not to thrive well together on similar anti-sane
and sanitized grounds together embrangled:
that is, the snowy campus discomfited

by the poets, unholy antecedents it—
the sanctosanct instistruction—
charges itself to kiln and shelve, that
Henry should leap to grace-lack swansong loondive.
Cannonball or bellyflop?

Poor ballistic, sad canonbawl.
Outside campus, out on, from any bridge—
Washington Ave, Harvard, Ferry St, *Orizaba*—
we are not expected to know what deaths to respond to.
But we are warned:

I'm too alone. I see no end. If we could all
run, even that would be better. I am hungry.
The sun is not hot
It's not a good position I am in.
If I had to do the whole thing over again
I wouldn't.   DS, 28
          *

We? or, well, *We? We* reck
ourselves respond to dimensions.
We respond: *we* turn
together to Henry's snowy prevision
and receipt, deceit—and recite,

69

then follow the nearest clearest photon *to*
yes, passing misunderstood,
Systems-settled in their Sockets —
yes, chastely re-defined cosmic laws
—resown with Colors . . .

settled in their Sockets —twisted in hard, then
wrenched into the machinery of the Spheres—
omniscient about art, music, architecture, sculpture,
and writers (ohmeohmy!)
and the Ocean—

the oceans, rivers, Earth, air, ionosphere,
the space-junqued Firmament,
the dulled music of tethered spheres,
the spheres polluted:
no, poisoned. The Bird—birds? . . .

Oh! Multicellular life! blasted to netherdom,
and human sensibility to its own existence may drop to
           near 0—
   Citadels—dissolved—

in the foresensible blind future
of the inexcusable past,
his head full
& his heart full, he's ready to move on   [DS 77]
and we who plod pages behind?—
        *

Once more, for this alone who may have returned:

The Dun Box

"And thus alas,
your state you much deplore,
In general terms, but will not say wherefore . . ."
                                                        Anne Bradstreet

The American Century,
that began on the deck of the USS Missouri
had already ended over Nagasaki.

The century may begin perhaps,
but not before the humble expiation
of its many false starts,
our eschatological hubris.

Some burning
in the burgeoning weathers . . .
If there were a middle
ground between things and the soul
or if the sky resembled more the sea,
I wouldn't have to scold my heavy daughter.   *DS 385*

To do right by Henry, Pussy Cat or Feral Fiend,
when context has gone extinct,
context attaches only to the lines that precede it
or to the comma and comet dash
on one side of a bridge or another—

                            Step, then, forth . . .

*Quotations from John Berryman in this poem:
Homage to Mistress Bradstreet, *Dream Songs,* and *Delusions, Etc.*

71

2. Wake Robin

Sleep realized
Was the whiteness that is the ultimate intellect,
A diamond jubilance beyond the fire.
      Wallace Stevens, "The Owl in the Sarcophagus"

Toad Shade

It is late May. It has rained
and the forest and the sky look feel sound taste
cold and sloppy.
Not enough sound to interfere with a sigh of devotion
in a self-inflicted chill wetting.

Clouds have begun to wilt into the eastern distance.
The lake has begun to warm to the new spring,
not enough
and no roar of pleasure-boats' displeasures.

Protected as well as I can be from the several
spring-bucked curses of tick,
out of some May-time folly
I slog through the final weeks of rot
from last fall's confused and wan
diminishment of summer life,
a ragged likfält, such fertile birthplace!

Somewhere under the rot,
rhizomes of trillium slither through thawed muck—
the distance of wishful thinking above
the muffled renewal of magma rising.

The Dun Box

In a couple of weeks maybe,
their stems will erect a ground-low canopy of green,
to support and sport pale clusters of white
blossoms ripening in the shade of senile aspens.

Before the end of their season trillium will solemnize
themselves into faded purple, a violet hour
of pretend Lenten-regal for the confusion
of any who require of plants the incense—
the condescending delusion,
the yoke and taint of blessing.
                 *

Until grass rises and the undergrowth greens,
this is a hillside the colors of a wet turkey—
                 *

My uncle planted the first trillium clusters decades ago.
Their travel by rhizomes underground,
slowly toward light and nourishment,
must be encouraged,
but only by meticulous inattention.
To pluck the flower is to kill the plant.

My uncle's plucked generation travels still
underground toward the fading or our memories—
more slowly for now—
then at once and not at all.
                 *

The plant in mute honesty abets only
our folksaga metaphors from ödmjuk runic alchemy—

toadshade, birthroot, wood lily, wakerobin.
Trille blanc in French, trilling in Swedish.

But Trillium grandiflorum is grand enough
to adorn the anthropo-genus
proprietary sanctum. The technician
tells no story. Folk names invite story.
Listeners invent story after story.

I do remember, as some days it was to me,
trilling like the hermit thrush.
Tempting our leaf-fledged delusion of a New Eden,
we know not to worry over
what we bless—only ourselves in grief.

      *

Non carpe diem, sed decerpta ex die.

The soar and talons of appetites
disjoined
may seize a day so long
or soon as days survive
for human grip to seize.

How much I would rather pluck
the fruits of my day, day by day
into the future of each day's given night,
as such goodness ripens
that I may have earned for tending
the dooryard of those futures.

For each of us, a day will be harvested
with all the next,
for some: seized—for whose survivors
condemned to a world of dis-ease,
fear-brewed hatred, the petty piss-off
of extinction-driven pique:

Real Notes

"They're real notes. Swear."
This from the girl with the blue clarinet.
Real blue. Swear.

Her notes are blue.
No metaphor. Swear.

What sound it is cannot be written out and out
and out as real notes, no more than whale song—
the real and ecstatic whale—
not the human's wistful echo of her many ghosts.

Or a wolf in the night,
keening its own extinction.
The soul-searching owl—
the soul-tearing rapacious owl.

A lone osprey's hard starving grief
having found no perch.
A death cry over dark water.
Real notes: silent.
The victory-smug burble of diving fish.

All notes. Swear.
The banshee-laugh of a siren
before a dread of dawn.
A tourist's drug-sweetened bliss
gaffed into madness.

The Dun Box

The note of nightmare howl
from the gutted mind
broils on the dream-flash rack
in the orchestra pit of refining flames—
real notes—hot licks.
            *

Now, now, now the death gurgle
of the man fixed flat on the pavement,
his neck pressed breathless, ground
under his killer's knee.
Loud sighs, muffled
outrage from intimidated bystanders.

Real notes, modulated.
Storm-stoked panic.
Primordial wail from the bereaved,
isolated beyond consolation.
The judge's footlit scripted blind deliverance:
his sentence of Original Guilt.

Nearly drained, in desperate modulation
the lover of death lowers the volume of notes.
Real notes. Swear.

The exhausted mother pleading so so so far
suspended beyond the graceless notes of language.
But real notes! Oh Swear!—

The squall-notes
of another summer aborning in surge—

death-march notes a dirge to mourn
a strangling new servility.
    *

Behind me,
back down the two-rut track and into the woods
echoes the flute-song of a thrush,
diminuendo.

Real notes. Swear. Only:
Once—upon a time.
Swear.

Birth Root

We might choose to remain below, behind,
just another mammal, really,
a short-lived species, swear,
as the evolution of species goes. And goes.

A primate, by the sullen grace of evolution—
as we also call our neglected, disparaged,
murdered, diminishing next of kin—
nearly hairless, possessed of a rich intellect,

condemned to understand the nature
of the suicide we may have casually doomed
ourselves to apprehend before the final blink.
Or. "If you can't say something nice . . ."

We after all and all, have too many reasons not to rise.
Or I have, anyway? And shall I ask around? Anyway?
Only a few reasons may ever be worthy
of the final slap into re-cognition—

at which, forest interrupting,
I remove a very small tick from my left calf,
almost panicked about a red stigma growing,
the bullseye rash of Lyme disease—
the emergency room, new symptoms, palsy maybe,
years of lingering debilitation maybe, maybe not—

still think to ask,
gesturing a bent finger into the cave of dank wood:
but what of the expanding life, rushing blood,

the flesh of us all— the hungry mortal harvest?
Food?
                *

A trillium's flesh wills to live on until
it happens to die.
Or it happens to live underneath
the feeding rot from last fall,

like you if you happen to burst
into the chill air again next spring.
If you—what? Live . . .

in words perhaps.
See from within layered glyphs,
figures on the cave wall.
Press your open hand.

Press an open hand
stained in something like blood,
something like words,
the corpuscles of the poem that just happens
to get spoken some night later.

Something like words
pressed into the side of a bison, say.
Then lift up, swear,
out into the radiance of spring
the bison and the words for and to the bison.

Yes, those words, and yes,
the very bison you will meet on the open ground.

All of those words—
the soul of them attached, inviting
the souls of other animals,

souls of comingling cells
in the words the bison, the aurochs, the cave bear
will follow the intelligence of white plants to their—

your shared surface on Earth running
with natural mind,
our shared world of folksaga, of

toad shade, birth root, wood lily, wake robin
trille blanc, trilling—
their colors, their ages and movements
from white to purple—to the ground we share:

birth root wood toad lily robin shade root birth,
a trill of new arrangement for each following spring.

A trill for the ultimate spring that follows only
into the wisdom of empty white, the purpling blossom.

Yes, but not swear. Nature
will not keep a promise she cannot make.

A New Kind of Light Again

The two storms in two days
that leave us a century or millennia
before electricity. No light anywhere.
Clear water, black in the night, soothing swish of waves
on the shore of the lake erase the much-too-present.

We dream-back the dark beginning again
before the advent of primordial blessing,
the murk of renewal
forbidden the rot-free polyethylene
human system fed for a century or two
on eons of black residue.

We scour similar residue from lamp chimneys, trim wicks,
remember, almost, how to adjust for smokeless light.
We haul water up from the backbreaking lake,
the heartbreaking drought.

We endure the inconvenience of slow machinery,
utterly trustworthy pain the modern neck
and we enjoy the reward
of the push and pull of it.

A yellow flame flicker of oil lamps
casts a softer reality than bottled light from bulbs,
like death-freed ancestors winking back
from the flickered history of their shadows.

Breeze-borne swirl of radiance
ridicules our industrious apostasy toward Life,

toward Nature, toward Spirits or Quanta,
all the imaginations we make into gods.

In welcome ancient gloaming we read poems,
eye-filling sensuous messages,
carboniferous, Earth-born
in their pencil-parsimony of eyestrain glow.

We read a poem, a thatched house in China
maybe, and maybe think, feel,
move to a languid flow of white,
and if a poem seems to fill mind and moment,
we can control the flame.

In that ancient light we share with poets,
we live out from the lines into the nurture,
the oneness of this reaffirming new night. In

the morning, light will return us
to the smell of gasoline from the lake,
panic-scream of horsepower and a sense of nothing
left for the production of sweet air or the light
of galaxies in our junkmurked heavens.

William Duffy's Hammock Was Strung
Between Two Trees

projected for the 2061 centenary of James Wright's poem

> *"I lean back, as the evening darkens and comes on.*
> *A chicken hawk floats over, looking for home.*
> *I have wasted my life."*

Well, now. Now? Sitting here in the shade
of air conditioning
in the middle of a prosthetic new century
what can I know now of William Duffy's farm?
Of William Duffy?

When have I last seen a farm
owned by someone with a human name? Or face?
When have I smelled hay inside
a pine-sided red-painted barn?
What do I know of Pine Island, Minnesota?

Are there still pine on the island? How many?
In what geography is the island, anyway? Is it
even an island in water? Is there water? Anymore?
How far must water be drilled
from under the barrens of farm country?

Minnesota went away.
James Wright carried it away
in the pocket of a denim freight car
on a frayed siding outside Fargo, North Dakota—
rails long since dragged to the Fargo Rust Museum.

The nature trail that replaced it has sported no footprints
since, since . . .
life
supported trees that supported hammocks
that supported any dream at all.

Richard Fenton Sederstrom

Measureless Float

I slowed the boat.
Light breeze guiding astern,
the lake asked us to drift
through a cold mist toward
what was no longer a floating pine bough,
large, dark with needles when we left the dock,
sunken now to rest low and flat on the surface.

The dark bough had turned
into a black shoal of mud hens,
coots, drifting ahead of us
toward some cloud-drowned shore.

Blind nowhere urged them to wait out
the few October days left them
before they would have to fly south,
or, iced in, fail ever to fly.

One coot popped into the air from an end of the shoal.
It flapped and dropped quickly.
Another popped up from the other end.
Then an eagle glided out of the mist above us all.

It flew over the shoal of little birds paddling in calm,
or calm panicked to a taut gun-spring.
The eagle veered and dove.
The eagle approached an end of the shoal
and another black snack flapped
up from the other end.

The Dun Box

The eagle aborted the dive, rose again,
and aimed toward the animate end,
but, from the end the eagle had first targeted,
another coot popped up and dropped.

None of them ever flapped high enough
that even the eagle might call it flying.
No bird offered a ballistic arc
for the eagle's ballistic response.
No bird presented itself as solid and true,
as Bird.

Again the eagle hesitated,
a Sky God confused, then rose,
adjusted for its target and trajectory,
and dove once more.

Another pop and flap.
Another aborted dive.
This continued.
A dive, a pop, from end to middle,
from middle to end, one or another.

We were as bewildered as the eagle
at the sight of small birds outmaneuvering
the taloned grace of Omnipotence.

Before I restarted the motor,
one of us may have said, thought,
that the better part of valor is no more than,
no less than the unthought insurrection,

almost imperceptible,
of nature's food-stuff—ourselves—
making way in maybe the last threatened world,
aggressive non-violence, shared life-wide
in patiently evolved resolution—

black shoal of common mud hens,
too common to notice at rest
nevertheless pop and flap up
into our shared range of intelligences.

No individual soul exists in
the kaleidoscope of helices, but only
the soul of common being that we share
in the chastening belly of Earth—

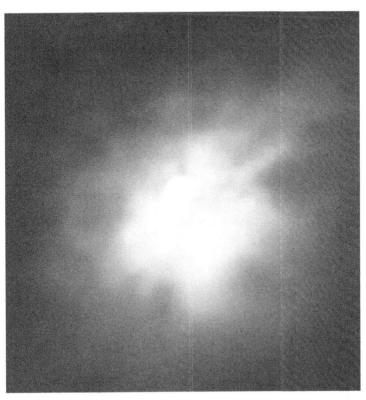

iii The Dun Box

Spring 1974

continuing straight ahead toward the line where the blue abyss
of Arizona falls away (just trying to think positive)
Franz Wright, "Through"

The fulsome Technicolor
sun-scape of early-morning mountain ranges melts.
We pass into mirages cut with rough triangles
of turquoise or lapis lazuli, diamond-incised
into eroding faces of escarpment.

After we have left them behind to melt
into tomorrow morning's new delusion,
the blind interstate lumbers down
and through dun foothills. Away from
the new sun, toward the Great Ocean rotting.

Dun hills sink toward the shallow dregs,
a reek of the Colorado River,
and the river looks back toward the flats of boredom
and a retro-neon interruption of small dry burgs
at the western border of Arizona, a stretch
of another flat, flat desert morning:

Sun. Pockets of housing, strip-lined stores,
and acres and acres of winter folk
identified by and with travel trailers,
RVs, and flea-markets. They glow in their agony,
blobs of hot-pink tattooing: cerise deep sunburn.
The Colorado River, once mud-red with native life,
dammed now, for decades turquoise green from above,

swimming-pool blue at the surface we drive by,
chilled from the dams—petty real estate now—

generations of lorn spirits poisoned, drowned,
the river, the dead brown god, sterile, laundry-blued,
seeming to signify not-quite-life, not-quite-death,
but despoiled, re-purposed, and merchandized.

Southward tan, dank in places,
crisping mud sloughed to insult Mexico, then
miles and miles and miles of the same beige
desert with a new name and no saguaro cacti.

We drive over the hot skin
of a dead black line in a touristical race
toward the tectonic edge of dire imagination.
                    *

Half alert to what we may have been talking about, or not, the
children seem protected again in a web of parental
responsibility defined by the necessary rigors in boxes of
expository prose. In no more than mechanical safety they
watch for the edge of the world, and they—
or Jackie mostly,

our bestirred elder daughter—are sleepily focused
on the looming eternal vistas.
What appear though are glaucous farm acres
boxed in squares around the town of Indio,
just past the last bit of world.
The streak of moss-green between road cuts widens
into a varied green patch-quilt in mottled shades of crop.

Carol turns around and mentions to the kids
something about how the land below is so different now,
to which Jackie, who has just turned "I'm six now," replies,
"Is that Land?!!"

Like the first little girl to cross the ice bridge
she is thrilled at the discovery
Land, Oh!! or in a peep of a child's elation: *Oooh!*
  *

Neil Armstrong looks
over to his co-pilot and announces that
they are about to land.
Jackie looks hard at the poxy surface of cold Moon
and asks back to Neil, "Is that Land?!!"

So much reality is made of circumstance and myth,
slowing what goes round to keep it from dying out.
The Mojave Desert, the Sonoran, the Moon:
it's all "that land?"!! in the jolt of discovery.

In the clutch of ownership it becomes "one small step,"
a clod of history kilned in marketing.
  *

Years later, seven-year-old Debbie declares
"O, look. It's just like England!" But it's Ames, Iowa.
Only it isn't Iowa anymore. It's England,
where she has never been—to her,
her grandmother's England in stories,
green and old and wholly present.
  *

How bare and wistless to correct and envy
in one sullen breath the child's regard for dreamscape
precision sprung from of her delight in images—

Spring 1863: to Vulcan's Iron, *introductory to myth*

The rut glimmered . . . .
I suppose it was trying to make some point
but we never found out about that . . .
John Ashbery, "Breathlike"

The desert road is graded, not recently.
Was smooth ever an issue? — Gold
is where glory soars, beyond the pomade of ease.

Decades past and past, *eureka!*-rapt, crawling
from hole to hole, rut to rut, rock to rock,
stumble to stumble, thorn to spine: mesquite
to paloverde to cholla to saguaro,
all decorate and arm the desolate fore-trails
to the expected comfort of traffic pattern.

Abandoned even from maps,
it is untrafficked, Anthropocene geology exposed,
a rut-designed monument dedicated
to viral existence and neglect in bland homage
to the human zeal for nowhere.
It goes there it seems, but where there?

The track and trace of it disappear
long before it might bother to reach the shadow-range
that screens the farther range after range
that disguise in their slow humor —
slow by the standards of our heroic fictions of life-span —
the willful bliss of a true horizon.
Am!
        *

From any spot on a spheroid, where is a true horizon?
That true horizon is also an illusion,
an hallucinatory effect of the reluctant kaleidoscope of
            tectonics.
Reduced to the size of a billiard ball,
would Earth be smoother than the newest 8-ball?

Would it feel wet? How could you tell?
We wonder for seconds when it started.
And to where it planned to travel.
It? It what? The road. The road planned?
It alone, unplanned . . . incoherent . . . La Sonora—
passing echo of the last quail-note.
Time, inchoate, pre-coherent, is the predicate.
            *

Or maybe only timing, unplanned, incoherent until . . . .
but It always is, which, a haze of pronoun,
like a Bartleby, a poet who will not be,
except in quantum regularity of ur-myth,
because as before, the same hour still proceeds barely
to nothing but another.

We would prefer not but always to live in the other.
Remember?
The next hour will never be more than an idea.

But it is not an unworthy one.
If not worthy, then no worthy idea can ever be,
especially to those of us who are not in it anymore,
who will not tell their survivors,

who, a ghost of quail to dream among, they sense
finally that time dissolves, as do aims. The where?
England? Sverige? The Moon? Iowa? Dao?

For now the note is a fossil of desert dirt-track, or no place.
Once it may have trekked prospectors to vast dreams
of a vaster shine of wealth. Only It.
Lorn pronoun underburdened by sound or sign.
Overwhelmed by wistless air. Sonora.

Before the mesquite on the left—a weed,
and sacred only to the free spirit of uselessness,
mule-trains may have dragged
the machinery of Earth-crunching
into the nowhere between here
and the light-embodied range before
that shadow-distance, the gray—or sepia
of a hundred-and-fifty-year-old photograph.
                *

Sepia is a shade for long aftermaths of funerals,
the shade of hair wreaths and aunts
disguised in their unbleached-straw-shade
nightgowns under sun-bleached sand—
in most of its colors, fading ecru.

That machinery may still rest somewhere.
To add dry-blood rust-red to the grunge of setting
the desert again gives the petrified ruts a focus
toward history of some future. Unpeopled.

The road? The futures?
The future imperfect and subjunctive.

Some creosote bush will have lived in clones for millennia.
In nine thousand years rust-blood-red blends still
in and with the beige and tan and dun and sepia—

(so many shades of the same shade) of desert sand,
toward the subjective mytho-history of Anasazi cities,
buried lumps of sun-kilned mud and broken pots.

    *

But then the glory-dream of gold in grungy rock,
a vein dream. All vain traces . . .
No: no traces. Only It again—or Us—in
the un-peopled geography now of empty track—

    *

fuels my nostalgia for the steam engine—
my wooden toy model of the De Witt Clinton—1831,
flying embers charred the clothes of passengers.

Like capitalism itself, it is assembly line tradition:
two sources of power to accomplish one job,
at 90 to 95 percent inefficiency. Institutional
corrosion.

Physics: the Avian View
with Signals from Walt
> *The scientists are in terror*
> *and the European mind stops . . .*
> Ezra Pound

The red-tailed hawk swoops. Hunting,
she neither accuses nor acknowledges.
She has no other business but her desert eyescape,
to keep the binding silence of her hunt.

Loitering in the creosote bush,
a lone quail uses the silence as a cue
to sing and yawp out his evolution
of invisibility among the cacti.

Dimensional perspectives are skewed in the sun.
Hawk and quail and I fail to watch
the road wander beyond the memory
of our thoughtless gratitude
for the feckless pleasure of passing broken relics,
toward any past we will not care to face.

American, United-Statesian, individual, united,
and forward *forward* **forward** squinting
into the western sun, we do not inquire into past pasts.

Our pasts, even yesterday as was,
are rootin'-tootin', all poised in the lens
toward the subjunctive cinematic future perfect.
But Fah! to forward foraging, all skewed.
We, you and I and . . . .

101

We, who if we will, also skewed,
depart again as quantum shade,
will not care or dare to observe meaningfully.
We may gander backward, gander sideward to
        *

the ones who walk beside you—
Titus Lucretius Carus, the Scot, John Duns,
inventing their way through the crazy maze
toward Richard Feynman's narrow horn gate
into every dimension of physics,
plans and models of separate and entwined—
who can know?—

futures that may involve you,
involve your ability to make choices
about your existence in the midst of,
on the edges of it—It—all.
        *

> I look up at the Cliffs
> But we're swept on by downriver
>   Gary Snyder

I look up too, as if in prayer
for the return to Nature of her gifts.
But I'm swept downtime–
the encyclopedic layers of cliffs are still below.

First the fox, gray fox, skittish,
as he should be, given his human company,

The Dun Box

then a gray-bellied osprey in a dead cottonwood.
I slow to watch the bird flap glare-blackened wings,
fall out of her innocence and become

the necessary predator
as she levels with the stream of narrow canyon air,
shoots the airflow above the last free river
in this desert state, plucks a small-mouth bass
and heads up-canyon. Not a sound.

At the riverbank I look up at the cliffs.
Above me in a cleft of canyon wall
a hawk's nest, a common red-tail.

I can just see the bullet scars around
the narrow slot, and on the ground below
part of a weathered wing.

I could try to bless this sad return
to tortured Nature of her gifts.
I could sprinkle a palmful of river water
on the few brown feathers, dry-blood-ochre sand,
the air-light fan of white wing bone.

But the water of this last free river in a desert state
has been rendered undrinkable,
rendered by our return to Nature
of her poisoned, gutshot gifts.

So I turn my back,
in leaving give such blessing as I can
by the promise of my human absence.

Wax wings melting aloft, black against the sun,
on behalf of the passing vulture I will practice
the vain and necessary rituals of grief—

Spring, 1974: Le Faye's Children

Landscape was never a subject matter, it was a technique,
A method of measure,
                    a scaffold for structuring . . .
            Charles Wright, "The Minor Art of Self-Defense"

For an hour's worth of attention on a flat,
straight, flat, flat, straight desert freeway
we alternate attention between ecru acres
shadowed by scattered creosote bush and debris—

and the gleam of blue diamonds showing right
and bright through the bulk of the solid
mesa ahead of our vacationing old beige Chevy,

sky-diamond windows sawn out of the broad
escarpment and growing broader and higher
and bluer—Vermeer's? Ah!—lapis lazuli bright,
angled, depressed into a Vermeer study
of my cube-quartered room-bound mind.

They close on us from the morning west.

Then the lazuli diamonds begin to open farther
into and against their gray background,
melt themselves and the mesa-tops out of
existence. The mesa is reborn
into a new mountain range, a small range,
but with teeth, like a lower jaw—hunger
painted by the amputated hand
of a clockwork prosthesis.

Richard Fenton Sederstrom

The young hills have sucked at the breast
of the mother mesa until she is devoured from below
and the shapely new range is weaned
into its fresh morning as another mirage,
an hallucination more confused.

The abdication of Belief
Makes the Behavior small—
Better an ignis fatuus
Than no illume at all. — — Again:
                    Emily Dickinson

We warp the stable world with our speed.
The whole range becomes a bump to the north,
then gone, like their swallowed mother,
not even a fleck in the rear-view mirror.

Belief is a capacity of physics,
the sacred *illume* of doubt—

Subjunctive Interruptions: Disneyland©™
Only If ?

> *Disney against the metaphysicals . . .*
> Ezra Pound, Canto CXVI

A century and a half ago we would have paled
in wonder at the shock of that solid
unmapped mesa that had not been there
only yesterday evening, or
can we remember at all?

And if we fail to trudge in reality any longer,
in the panic of so many kinds of thirst,
what use is a map?

Still, we surely would have studied the map again,
and maybe we would have changed
our direction, to the south maybe,
and a vastness of desert, at the pace of horses'
mesmerizing walk, a geological nightmare
far deadlier than this one.

And maybe by the time the sun had revealed
the truth of mountain
out of the mystery of mirage,
we might already be dying, untracked,
in sere wonder, then
dust-drowned and desiccating
out of our illusion into truer madness—
then leatherbound dust mummified.
　　　*

But ours is only a brief vacation,
a weekend on the coast a few hours west.
The car follows the black track of highway,
past mirages no more now than an entertainment
of invented memory.
In the back seat, our three children see only Disneyland,
all in their six sense receptors:

Disneyland ©™ !!!

For their lorn parents the road
reflects back like ice-sheen,
silver-black, brittle,
deadly in the sun.

Our kids are sheltered by the clear and right-angled
definitions of ninety degrees for every corner of boxed prose,
as though I have invented a bomb-shelter for children and
futility, square-framed and right angled, protected as though
in the immoveable light of the ordinary Vermeer room, where
the warmth of sunlight is organized in the glaze of mortal
geometry, a safe universe, mortal and immortal according to
the inhalations of the undying day,

outside, where the painter kept himself alive
until after *Rampjaar*, art and life suffocated
by the ill-chance of war.

We can move from the one obvious peril
to peril that is all tawny glow, claws hidden,
the mirage of spirit that we carry

to light our trepid way toward
every cotton-candy shadow, toward
the teeth of more malicious goblins.

We may refine the daily jolts
of necessary care into poetry,
by the accident of nursery rhyme
move the life of words into worlds
of close and closeted meditation.
But the rote mechanics of raising children is prose.

Is this a poem about responsibility? But isn't
chore responsibility a matter for lists in prose?

Is this then a poem about prose, and if so,
does it extol prose, or as both
does it embrace the natural rigors and blind
fears that belong to the far ancestral enigma,
ain ma?

By which torch-lit chthonic depths
does it return to a poem about poetry?

Or is the *essai* Everyperson's reminder of, the *exagium*,
aliento opening the frail boundary between—
no, before such distinction could be made
between ritual and exposition—
cave wall and chalkboard?

Is it our preparation for the projective
co-relative magic of our heading,
a poem of some sort to seal our trust

in my nether-course ability
to engage nightmare, *comme dans*
le tombeau, while I fend off goblins,
highway patrol radar,
and eighteen-wheelers

and while our children contemplate the plastic anticipation
of half-life on Main Street (1890s Ames, Iowa?)
and the town's well-swept radiations out,
expanding Everychild's dream of candy-coated autocracy,
without restriction or meaning, except
for mouse-tail rubber thorns in the cartoon briar-patch?

For adults it is another experiment in blind perspective
where we watch realized virtuality play out in Technicolor
on the polished streets, veneers of the United State of
                    Americana
or we participated:
              *

—as when we got trapped on the closed Monorail car
through three laps of the route, happily forgotten
by the bland blind American-istic gleam
radiating between the Mouseployee's cap and uniform.

But the Monorail is electric. It is a train.
In the U. S. of Americanica? AutoNation?
It must be an illusion.
No one notices!
To misjudge the improbable saving genius
at a slow quiet pace is embarrassing
to the institutionalized mentality.
That's us, one or the other.

The Dun Box

—as when once I asked my five-year-old son
after we spooked the Haunted Mansion,
"Were you scared?"
Tom nodded then and said, "No."

But the thrill had offered something urgent for his mind,
and while he was dealing with it, I asked, "Tom,
if your ghost helps you flush here at Disneyland,
will you help your ghost flush at home?"

Influenced by Disneyland's animousy magic,
the automatic urinal flushed magically right then.
At the motel, Tommy helped his ghost flush three times
in five minutes. I stopped him. We talked.
A father's good ideas are always good;
they don't work very often.

We live in our deserts, I am dryly reminded.
We flush water.
Some golf, bushwhack through coiffured jungles:
plod on rich grass in soggy courses.

Pipes drip; some of us fix them. We adhere
to inherited dust bowl atonement: conservation—
two of the more delicate and will-o-the-wisp chimeras:
moderation and soul, however withered.
*

—and as when once we watched an arrest happen
in a line nearby. If you open your eyes
you can still see the blank climate of No.

No one in the line reacted.
Not one seemed to notice at all.
Is Justice blind, or merely undetectable?
Citadels dissolved.

What can be said about infotainment justice
when what passes for evidence of its practice
is not examined even in the static
excitement of an unmoving queue unnoticed?

Virtuality will not be intruded upon
by the unreality of actual occasion.
The sudden gap in the line is always swallowed
out of anticipatory existence, like the end-notated
small-print digestion of historicians:

the dire comforts of the desensitized elect:
law-abiding orthodoxy,
well-swept impartial parking lots
and lots of impartial fresh paint.

Much complaisant waiting in the California glow
under the grace of its beige firmament—
The celluloid of it all! But—

Spring 1974 to 1863: Postlude

—for now and for the 400 or so minutes of our trip
roaring by so slowly,
confined as we are only by road, time,
and the illusory horizon and freed
from the hallucinations of timeless
space by the hallucination of safety at freeway speed

and fast-frame moments of eroding geology
into the passing hallucination
of mountain peaks and dark mesas,
I accelerate to meet and pass the illusion of going

back somewhere graded, not recently
but decades or pages past and past.
From hole to hole, rut to rut, rock to rock,
stumble to stumble, thorn to spine: mesquite
to paloverde to cholla to saguaro,

all decorate the soul-ripening alternatives
to traffic pattern: from all points on a sphere
there *are* true horizons, perhaps not exterior to dream.

The poet's calling is to keep
dimensions of horizon in and out of sight,
to move behind a lens bouncing
from rut to rut toward a focus of bleeding
touch from thorn to spine:
share the human zeal for going
nowhere, to discover in the ultimate note,

another tangent, Us again, la Sonora,
still to invoke chase-and-recover.

But slow. We are learning, as the ancestors
knew from the ashen taupe, the Earth-borne dun,
the neutral cosmos of their cockcrow senses—
before the very first wheel-rut was pressed,
before all Earth be rutted and ransacked—

how to journey in space in spinning place, deep and,
without leaving another rut or even footprint,
to learn not only how to journey in place or no-place,
but to idle—

like perch gently fanning calm lake water,
feeling the fin-made current against
my swaying source-starved body,
limbs resisting the cool push of water
in treasured place and measured time,
time permitting—or time remaining . . . but
again, from any spot on a spheroid,
where are true horizons?

True horizons are also internal,
hallucinatory effects of the draught of mirage—
deep deep blue, obsidian cold,
breathless depths where we dare not drown—
nor will we drown even if we dare,
in the dun dry sand, welter and waste
of our sacred first delusions—

but the light signs eternal
a pale fire over marshes
 where the salt whispers to tide's change
Time, space,
 neither life nor death is the answer.

*

One day we, or such as may survive us,
must find out the point of the glimmered rut
we have never found out about—that . . . but—

Dun, Undun

—never

in time

               never

                         to completion

 jamais

                          une fin

ever

à l'heure ,

                 jamais

                      le hasard

      Le Fantasme *ala*

            UN COUP DE DÉS

            gaming gamely *avec* Mallarmé

    or/*et avec* Ol Ez—

a little light, like a rushlight
         to lead back to splendour

   . . . or Fata Morgana:

like the poem,

The Dun Box

the living will in the wisp:

the path of any electron:

the sea, toward thee I roll   . . .

*

But I love delicacy   and this to me —
the brilliance and the beauty of the sun — desire has allotted.

i.e. it coheres all right . . .   (E.P.)

mais non:
            tu me regardez
Je ne peuz te dire
encore la vérité
            je n'ose, trop petit
Ce qui t'est arrivé   (S.M.)

but no: I cannot tell you the truth.
Can I ever more dare, mes petits,

                        jamais, jamais mieux?

in the book, or the mad prophet, or, no . . . under, but

117

Once more:

What a wonder of imagination,
that having discovered that we can't control what is—
the tides, the weather, the migration of wildebeest,
the behavior of our children or the clan in the next forest,

the gravitational pull among planets, stars, photons and quarks,
the vatic fecklessness of poets—

we turn to a faith in our power to control
what we know to be ephemeral: confessio infidelitatus—
*

wait . . . for now

nor in the innocence, nor even the silence,
       but the silence far
              what sound does the whale
make from the, from the, or is it
      the pure white light sounding sounding
           sounding
        the futile rattle of dry pages in an
attic-worn volume, the volume of white clouds of heavy
      invisibility
      left to the last breath of the final
      reading
          or flash of
                fin

118

Am

I getting anywhere by now?
Any where? Any now?

Missed a shade of sameness? Ignored
a smoked-out haze of taupe in the USian dream?

I rather hope not, not now.
I'd not care to lose some blur in the edge of myself

or of Bartleby in the tedious enthusiasm
for achievement.

Not now, yet
no, no never we prefer, because
    *

ever is, or is perhaps the speedily abbreviating
world of my beloved children,

steeled by the indomitable never of our aspirations—
gentle children,

my offspring, my heritage, and,
but it will be well never

to have told them, or me:
my fated accomplices. *À jamais . . .*

iv Far Shores, Closing

avlägsna stränder, stängning

For Nick Salerno

Proem

Note to the Office of Interpretation
      For Nick Salerno, *magister ludi*, who
      to my regret never visited these places.

I am delivering the enclosed ideas to you,
four of them so far, maybe five.
I anticipate that each of the ideas
is connected to the other three, or four.

I will not bore you trying to explain the connection
even if I thought myself worthy to do so.
Besides, each idea will explain at least part
of one or more or all of the other ideas.

The first idea is the trillium, ageing into Lenten purple,
      alone under a dying aspen.
The second idea is that morning in April that rose
      like a yellow cactus blossom over the bay in Guaymas.
The third idea is a knot in a pine wall, the one just above
      the homely lamp made of a cholla skeleton.
The fourth idea is what we just saw run out of
      the screen door letting it slam, as usual,
      a riotous pentecost.

One idea can never stand alone, so you say.
But if one idea *must* be supported
by at least one other idea, in their mutual support
they may speak only to one another, like poet to poet,
      player to player, soul to soul.

And finally to anyone outside cloister or workshop
welcome to a sense of new ideas.
Inside scholastic cryptophilia, whatever is
is only another pebble to kneel on, to prove
          the breathless scruples of the lapidary imagination.

But outside! Ah.
Yes, there is a fifth idea.
Just there. And there as well.
That multiplex world,
          everywhere you and I have spoken.

More of Us

Nick Salerno, who taught me write from wreck
or droit from dreck, would've gone loopy
at this in-and-dis-sequential sequence and loopier
at my use of "loopy" in something like public. You,
"Old enough to be . . . your, O—Big brother?" And so—
        *

And I mention Hugh Fenton without explaining,
again. Nor will I explain now.
And, impudently again, I twist Nick about,
in my Ariel job to tease more his dear memory:
Some tricks of desperation: a scar of quietus.
        *

Du Fu is the lornsome Chinese poet most venerated,
and I have no Chinese;
but I have a bit or touch, a schmear of poet. And
        *

who says Eumaeus is a fictional character?
If we choose to agree that Homer is not fictional,
Homer having left no records on papyrus
or even scratches in the sand of beaches—
well, academic hunches way aside—

if Homer can speak to Eumaeus, any poor poet
can speak to Eumaeus, *the only figure in all of Homer*
whom the blind poet addresses: "you." "You speak."
I have dared speak before with/for Eumaeus. And so:

125

Richard Fenton Sederstrom

Words with the Orthodox

In his moment of errant confidence
Heraclitus declaims

—now we can travel anywhere!
No longer must we lug the poets
and mythmongers along for stubborn witness
about indisputable certainties. —

Stretched out in the morning sun,
Eumaeus scratches his dinner behind the ear
and says, but not aloud

Now that we know that however far
we travel we are in the vastness:
nowhere yet,
how can we hope to arrive without
poets and oracles for mused
witness among disputed facts?
                    *

Heraclitus:
The soul is unfathomable
though examined for ages
to a depth beyond report —
Eumaeus:
while the poet's words
explore breath by breath to
a report beyond depth —
                    *

The Dun Box

They say that the sun has been
865,000 miles wide, give or take,

almost all the long eons since its birth.
To Heraclitus the sun is one foot wide.

In another two and a half millennia
will the sun be that much narrower

by geometric measure and moral erosion
or humans that much smaller?

Will humans then be able to see
the sun as it is, or ourselves as we are?
                              *

Eumaeus:
Be all that you are or can be!
Be rich!
How can any fate be direr?
Unless you also long for power.

Richard Fenton Sederstrom

Moods:

Indicative

Charles Wu and I were talking.
Charles was a scholar and translator of Laozi.
I offered my preference for Zhuangzi.

Diane Ma asked me in some shock, "Zhuangzi?
Not Laozi? How can that be? But why?"
"Because he reminds me of my grandfather."
She had no response. Charles smiled.
Charles and Zhuangzi require no more to say.
I failed to ask for Laozi's comment.

It's an ancient smile, that response
from out the pictured cave into the sun.
In that primatial sun I have four grandfathers now.
Maybe five, one of whom may be myself at long last.
We try to speak through one another.

Eumaeus, Zhuang Zhou, Du Fu, Hugh Fenton,
me; dynamos of passivity, companions of the dao
of necessary occasions—as they arise.
It takes all four, or five sometimes,
but who is the other?

Subjunctive

Again, of late, again—again must I have so
wearied . . . wearied stark . . .what?
my soul? Souls? Just words.

128

The Dun Box

What is a poet's soul but just words?

For the day, perhaps,
which soul or shadow of my own I should invite
along with my grandfathers' souls:
Hugh Fenton, Zhuang Zhou, Du Fu, Eumaeus.

And our shared retreats—
Log-slab covered tar-paper cabin. Folly.
Thatch-roof cottage. Piercing absences.
Stone hut and pigsty, maybe interchangeable.

Deep blue lake, ciscoes jumping,
forest shadowed, green.
Shaded valley lakes and streams, sacred mountains,
crags, clouds.

Hills guide down to luffed sails
in a clearwater port—
to loaf together, diddling our toes
in a bright sea of pregnant wine.

The necessary condition of our apartness
ought to keep us close and closed together
in mutable cloud-bound arrangements, stories,
the antics we share in syllables and silences
radiated out from within our kaleidoscopic
pirouettes of mind waiting for shared rhythm.

Our communication, even scattered here,
should have been distinguished, one voice
from the others. That may not be.

Our core of years, our witness, growing
as one and another in one or another fluky voice
to witness in our shared days and ages,
axial treasures of thought and spirit: cultures—
thrush and flute songs: the music!

And wars, treacheries far gone and near.
Castles, basilicas, laws of trebuchet and bomb.
Survivals: Permian. Cretaceous. Anthropocene?

. . . O, and the good of waiting.
Keeping the table ready for twenty years or ever:
we also serve . . . and ever.

Our shared life longing for the company of friends
and cabin-comfort if not property
and fated instead to apartness and the failure
that is both Circe and Penelope to the unrequited poet:

Even together, with our, my dis-chordant tongue,
we would stammer toward . . . and avoid the epode
as we avoid, without resistance, finality.
Not alone any longer, but together,
doglike we could circle the habitat.

Conductive:

    Hugh Fenton
Our shared decision at Gettysburg.
Melancholy.
Buying solitude with Yankee peddling.

The love of language,
the pain of having to employ it merely.

Hugh:
After Gettysburg,
I could never leave my comrades,
but I never fired another shot.

Thank God I never had to.
I don't know what . . .

You know what your problem is, Richard my lad?
Your problem is . . . well
you don't hold your mouth right.
You've got to learn to hold your mouth right.
            *
Can we strive for clarity
in the end of our work and our words—
the embodied silence
from which another might create new clarity?
Is it hard trying to get lost
even in battle
because of the efforts of observing,
the need to discover what
is new in the beckoning wordscape
of lostness?
            [from *Sorgmantel*]
            *
 Zhuang Zhou
Some admonition might Zhou give here
casually to ward off disaster to the ambitious,

131

from the shadow now of his westering way,
the crumpled silk of his small fame.

from Zhuangzi, in Tomas Merton's version:

What do you think? Is it better to give up one's life
and leave a sacred shell as an object of cult
in a cloud of incense three thousand years,
or better to live as a plain turtle
dragging its tail in the sand? Go home!
Leave me here to drag my tail in the mud!

In my way I follow the master's indirection,
avoid intent. Pelt stretched here, wrinkled there,
balding and baggy-eyed, I have subtly avoided
the eight by ten glossy by way of the program
                    of unstudied inaction.
          [from *Icarus Rising*]
             *
          Du Fu
We share drink, depression, diabetes
and you, a long slog to Zizhou. I?
Dirges to conscripted dead, their wives and children.
Laments for his own.

On sore feet to see the family alive, mourn lost son.
Ambitions razed by private genius:
sounds of words in images.
Hanzi emerge from the dao of the brush.

from Du Fu, in David Hinton's version:

Bamboo chill drifts far into sleep. Wildland
moonlight fills our courtyard's every corner.

heavy dew beads and trickles. Sparse stars
kindle Presence—then darken into Absence.

Fireflies in dark flight flash, flash. Lingering
night out on the water, birds call back and forth.

All things caught between shield and sword,
all grief empty—the clear night passes away.

response from a distant generation:
Two loons outside lake-glow
coo to each other about migrating

and the tiny music of a small fish
flipping on the surface of the lake—
far outside the ammo-racket of civil mayhem
and the dis-civil ranting of demagogues.
I rise in some quiet hunger outside aliment.
Moon-glow glides toward us and fades.
      [from *Sorgmantel*]
       *

Eumaeus
We, you and I, still share longing for the sake of . . .
well, of longing. What spares the length of hours.
Keeping the table set and lorn lights on Ithaka.
Loyalty is a louche form of allegiance
raised by soul to hospitality.

from Homer, and Eumaeus:

You answered him, swineherd Eumaeus—Eat
dear guest, enjoy it, simple though it is.
Gods give, gods take away, as is their will:
to gods all things are possible.
     Emily Wilson's version
      *

 Mindful Eumaeus,
you are the one left surviving to assist us to remember
the voices of the poetry—when no god is listening.
While the gate of horn is open, speak—
     [from *Eumaeus Tends*]

in the storyful hospitality of long-past
and reapproaching occasions:

the timelessly available
Eumaeus, whose table waits for us.
I'll be there too. Maybe the others.
Maybe not; you never know nor need to.

We'll eat.
Well, we'll eat and talk.
In the morning maybe we'll walk down to the pier.
Watch white sails take to the sky.

Tentative Reverence

Mostly silence, anticipations at rest.
We share moments, not solemn—still though,
the still sad music: reply to the echoing
rumble of Nature, snoring deities.
Or we try, I with pen and paper.

We share our singular and personal secrets
in silence, in order that what is most to us,
what we'd prefer not to we still prefer
and proffer in silent rhythms—wing-beats
of an owl in our earliest dawn-lit forest—
     *

James Wright and Apollinaire pray together
as translator and poet—as poets together—

Apollinaire in Wright's English:
"All we want is to explore kindness, the enormous country
 where everything is silent."

And Wright added aloud,
"Christ, I'd rather have written that than go to heaven."

Sometimes we share words that might be heaven.
     *

Four—six? more?—of us alone together,
not without enlisting company,
crowding centuries. Longing

for we are poets of longing. Longing, *langian*
and lucky in words, in the vagaries of Fortune's Folly.

In our fortunes
we have long grown accustomed
to our incubate distances:

horizons bound by centuries
and opened into aeons splattered
into dollops of tempera, mosaic shards,
marble chunks, and papyrus
ready for planting, painting or words and words.

Sandbox and mudpies: ghosts at play,
modeling the *bas-relief* strata,
prepared negatives of the souls of Earth.

Evolution is home, where we keep our books,
our pens and strata of paper,
all the accoutrements
that with chastened mind add up
to our battered blabbing soul
opened to shared dimensions.

Just words,
no less than just.
This single stammering entity,
four out of how many more?
How many fewer?
Our disheveled universe is how large?
Is how small?
And how all in between?

The Dun Box

Time is the subjunctive predicate,
immaterial, that may propose the connections,
justify the aeons, should vouchsafe gravity
to what seems undiscoverable:

as we may do to summon and weigh the gods,
our self-arrayed, self-arraigned deities—
we approach our ordinary arts
with tentative reverence.

It's fair, as long as we digest only one another.
I could believe in a god or two who can't bite,
some gods' self-created grace of inner control. But
what I have seen in the created dark is all truth—

and I am comforted if we agree to absorb each other
quietly—bound gently among the Moirai—
and if we agree to the only authentic prayer,
inquisitive expression of devout skepticism.

It is self-reflective reverence of course,
because the gods deserve such attention
as befitting the human exempla their human creators
instilled or distilled in the colors of their natural
misbehaviors—

With tentative reverence toward
the foolscap adventure of home,
such security as we think we may deserve,
the same fen-and-street-soiled, half-chastened mind
that adds up its cirrus-shadowed selenity;

if we are so curb-chastened
maybe we will fail to grow accustomed
to the incubus loneliness:
*from the cheerful ways of men
cut off.* The blindness visible.

The collected mind alone
meditating the ways of gods
we create as though coordinated,
daily agreed in common distance
to grow in isolation together,
will fail to acquiesce to forces assembled
against this foolish phantom insurrection.

Last First Persona

Is any phantom exorcised?
Should be?
Is memory,
phantom understood in our projective longing
to live beyond and beyond and beyond?
Or the poem?

I have consulted the Eliots,
George and Tom on the subject,
and I correspond with Mallarmé,
who will convince me —
and I am wraithful glad —
that the poem's authenticity digests the poet.

But I am not yet convinced.
I am more than not untempted.
Lowell is on the alimentary side,
but Cal, Theos' bound enthusiast,
(whoever Theos might be) —

not ever the steadiest authority--
but my own not-so-distant mirror,
still a sad old man trying to pretend
to be a sad old man — a trick
he can't quite pull off, we can't,
the act being true.

Richard Fenton Sederstrom

The Light We Earn

"We, but how many are we?
In willful thrall to the music, we struggle our way
not to peace, but toward tomorrow
the thirteenth day"
the epiphany relived that, inside the poem,
time proceeds to nothing but:

growing up, slowly, never finally.
I may learn to live in the words we few share.
The talk that precedes does,
by something like definition, move, or vibrate,
drawing me to follow,
or contest my years of constriction,
to play within our chosen rings and bounds.

But if in its office of preceding we can move nowhere,
still we share a mutual intuition of electrons,
time's athletic Ariels, mortals' time-mates.

Perhaps the elegance of equation does proceed in time,
on the cave wall, but with no rune for the one hour to proceed,
time will not move, so it may not proceed. In time.

But I can imagine, in breathed timespun movements.
The next hour cannot come, cannot be,
but if I am, I live only this being:
a single continued existence. This day.
Nor can the object be that we cannot obtain,
out of any time that cannot be.

The Dun Box

We several together connect our centuries.
Something we want more than to believe is "time."

But time measured in static units,
like the hour we search for,
may be measured as well in the steps we take,
the words we practice, our morning appetites,
on the way down the trail to the sea.
White of sails.

Time starts, then slows, while we slip bare feet
into the blue water cold beneath the dock,
while we forge words we need to interrupt,
while talk itself continues, in its own predicates,
to postpone the quantum predicate,
time joins time. Then we eat.

If one hour proceeds, shared,
it maintains its own cell in time,
desk, paper, mind, forcing ahead and ahead the time

we would prefer to challenge, day by day,
the trepid empty feeling of sensing where we are when:
the fear-born confirmation
that we are in the only hour ever possible
in each single hour we dream
and invest with our breath.

The next hour need bring to hand
no more than a poem,
or my share in it.

Richard Fenton Sederstrom

We aim to do the thing for good.
If we must do it over and over again—
we must and will and will—
we do it now, each try,
and we do it for forever—
until the next time, only in order

to unite our stammered ages of dialogue—
each shared meeting, every simple meal,
each word, each gesture—and do it forever.
Until the next time beyond.

Any horizon, like time,
constricts the habitat—
                    *

The late-day sun shines out the adagio
of branch-latticed snow, chanceled light
for a motif to introduce the physics,
the gravity of theme
in the place we need revealed to us

for no longer than the hours
when the music and the silence swell
to become a return to the first moments of sharing—
the composer, the poet, the gift of
the music, the words,
a concerto of distant figures in time:

mouths, ears, wood, sinew, pen and ink—
hands working in the clays of notation:

sounds to relate the works of hours,
the newborn rhythms of any final day.

Then *a little light* again maybe.
The sea, the moon almost *like a rushlight* . . .
guiding inward *sine proprio*—
else, what? Bartleby? *Toward thee? Ad silentium.*

Ah. Anatole:

Le père cherche—	The father looks —
et s'arette—	and stops —
l'enfant étant	the child being
la, encore, comme	there, still, as if
pour reseize la vie	to take hold of life again
—or interruption	—now interruption
chez la père—et la	in the father—and the
mire apparue espoirs	mother appearing hopes
soins— le double côté	cares — the double side
homme femme	man woman
—tantôt chez	—soon in
union profonde	profound union
lune, chez l'autre, d'où	the one, the other, from which

Stéphane Mallarmé, *Pour un tombeau d'Anatole*
trans. Paul Auster.   [fragments]

143

Richard Fenton Sederstrom

All the Rules

Because you are, whoever you are,
I call out, "Rule Number One!"

From the precipitance you have adopted—
tree, boulder, high bank above the lake,
you call back to me, "No Bleeding!"
And you do not bleed, at least today.

Because you are, whoever you are,
I call out, "Rule Number Two!"

From that depth of the lake, the depth
almost above your head, you poke
your nose into the air and call back
"No Drowning!" And you don't, today.

Because you are , whoever you are,
I call out, "Rule Number Three!"

About to step into the poison ivy
to retrieve ball, frisbee, or arrow
you call back to me as you reach,
"No Scratching!" And you withdraw.

You know, at least for this time,
what rules direct the rules, and you
know that your job is to translate
what I say and create what I don't say.

The Dun Box

What I shout makes meaning for a minute.
What you think on your own creative
self sometimes keeps you from falling,
from drowning, from itchy agony,

and maybe from keeping someone else
from bleeding, drowning, even scratching,
maybe because you stop to think and care.

Because we listen together,
I don't have to explain or demand.
I don't have to invent Rule Number Four.

You know it for both of us. Or, no. You
know it for the kinship we may all become.

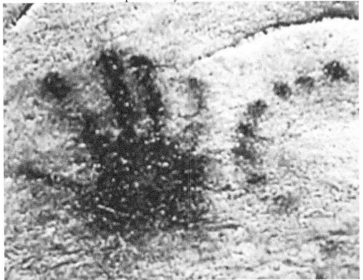

envoie: edge

When the saying ceases to be pleasurable
I'll probably stop.

When the saying becomes too much pleasure
maybe I'll cease.

Maybe I'll wonder in my coming dotage,
if this is so good what can I find that may be better?

Trying to find an answer
I may forget to speak the final question.

Then I'll have nothing left to utter in answer
when I address the life-worn sill of whereafter.

      *   *   *   *

We are creatures of Edge—sea and shore,
forest and savanna, oasis and desert,
cave and starlight, moon and sun.

Never ever only one or the other,
nor ever quite both.

    *

Aspiration is gray:

Made in the USA
Monee, IL
09 October 2023

44267170R00094